THE

FAMILY TREE

OUR FAMILY TREE
NOTEBOOK

Greetings Family Historian,

Our Family Tree Notebook was designed to look like a matched set when paired with *Our Family Tree Index* (the world's first-ever 12 generation family tree notebook).
It can also be used as a stand-alone notebook to preserve your genealogy notes in style.

Whether you use these pages to record remembered stories, interviews, family recipes and traditions, research notes, or records of genealogical sources, the leafy areas at the top of the pages can be used to write in the index numbers or the names of any relatives mentioned on the page, for quick reference. You can paste in photos, census and newspaper clippings... old lace... you can be creative and make this book truly yours.

This notebook was created at the request of the professional genealogists who loved the 12-generation family tree index book in this series, and needed more room to write about their discoveries.
Thank you all for the encouragement and support!

The pages are acid-free, and you are encouraged to write with an acid-free pen (available at any art store) so future generations will have a chance to enjoy your contribution to the family's history.

Yours Truly,
House Elves Anonymous

P.S. A CREATIVE TIP: If there are any pages you don't need, you can use a glue stick to attach a beautiful envelope to the page. This is a great way to store mementos! You can find a vast variety of unique print & fold envelopes in the Free Library at PegasusPaperCo.com

CONTENTS

A chart showing a handy numbering system for 8 generations of ancestors.
You can write each ancestor's corresponding number at the top of any pages that mention them.
Lined note pages with a different design in each section.
2 genealogy reference charts

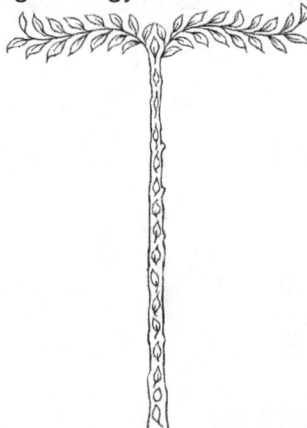

HOUSE
ELVES
ANONYMOUS

This notebook is dedicated to the Ossip, Gonek, Drahos, and Caplan families, with a special welcome going out to the new arrivals. Thank you for sharing an abundance of diverse curiosity and deep kindness. And to Aarti, Katherine, and Esther. Because chosen family is just as important, and we'll always have Paris. With love, S. Zar

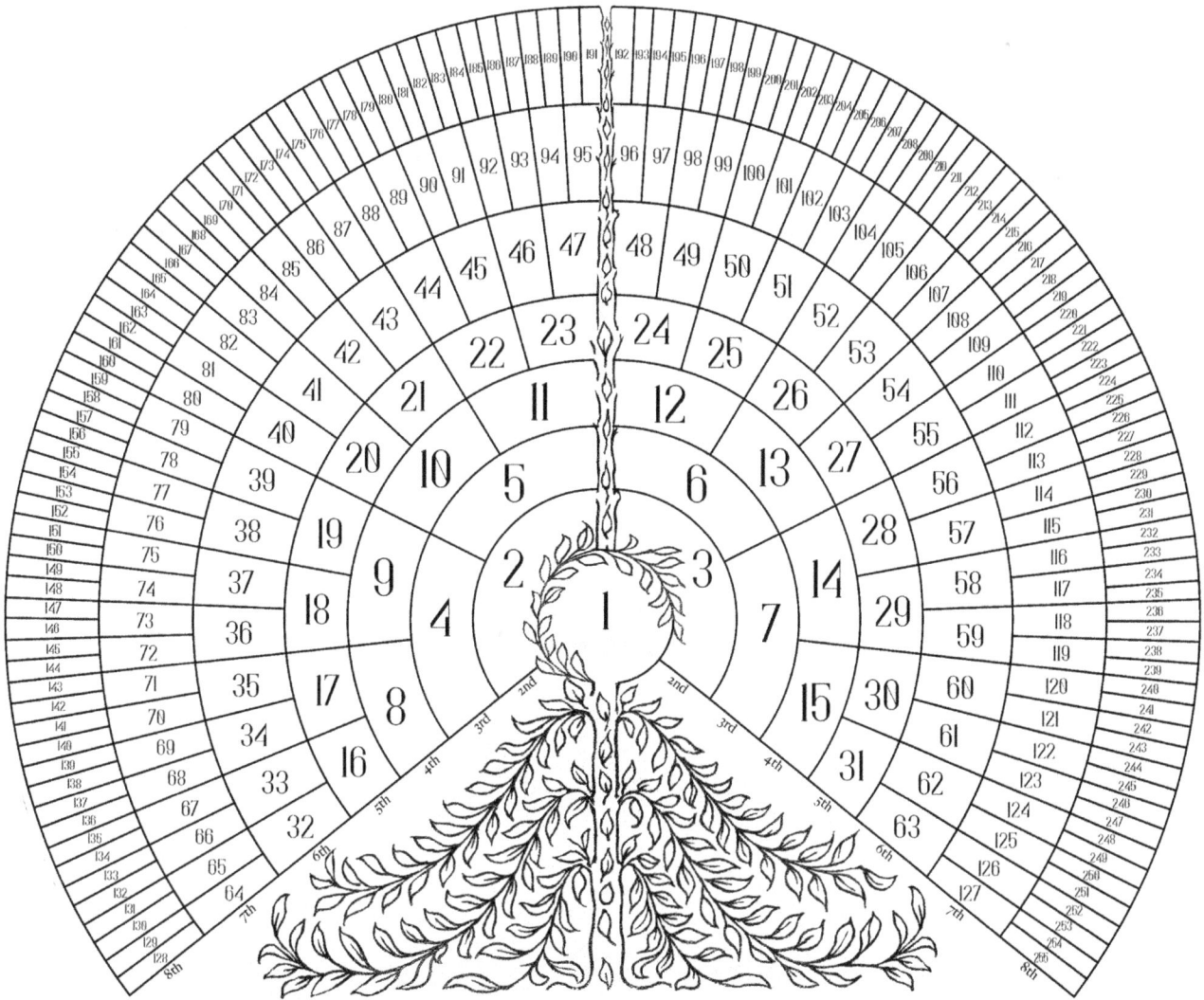

INTRODUCTION

HOW TO USE THIS FAMILY TREE BOOK

Each number in the tree above corresponds to an ancestor in your family tree. (There are larger versions of this chart on the next page and at HouseElvesAnonymous.com, where you can download it for free.)

Recording your family history is a deeply personal and meaningful adventure, and this book strives to give you as much free-writing space as possible. You can write in things like interesting historical notes, occupations, favorite quotes, hobbies, or how a couple first met and fell in love.

If you are looking for more guided ways to enhance your research, you can join my newsletter for some free printable reference gifts, or find family tree research tools in the shop at HouseElvesAnonymous.com

1

2

3rd
2nd

4

5

8

9

10

11

4th

16

17

18

19

20

21

22

23

5th

32

33

34

35

36

37

38

39

40

41

42

43

44

45

46

47

6th

64

65

66

67

68

69

70

71

72

73

74

75

76

77

78

79

80

81

82

83

84

85

86

87

88

89

90

91

92

93

94

95

7th

128

129

130

131

132

133

134

135

136

137

138

139

140

141

142

143

144

145

146

147

148

149

150

151

152

153

154

155

156

157

158

159

160

161

162

163

164

165

166

167

168

169

170

171

172

173

174

175

176

177

178

179

180

181

182

183

184

185

186

187

188

189

190

191

8th

The
Ancestors of

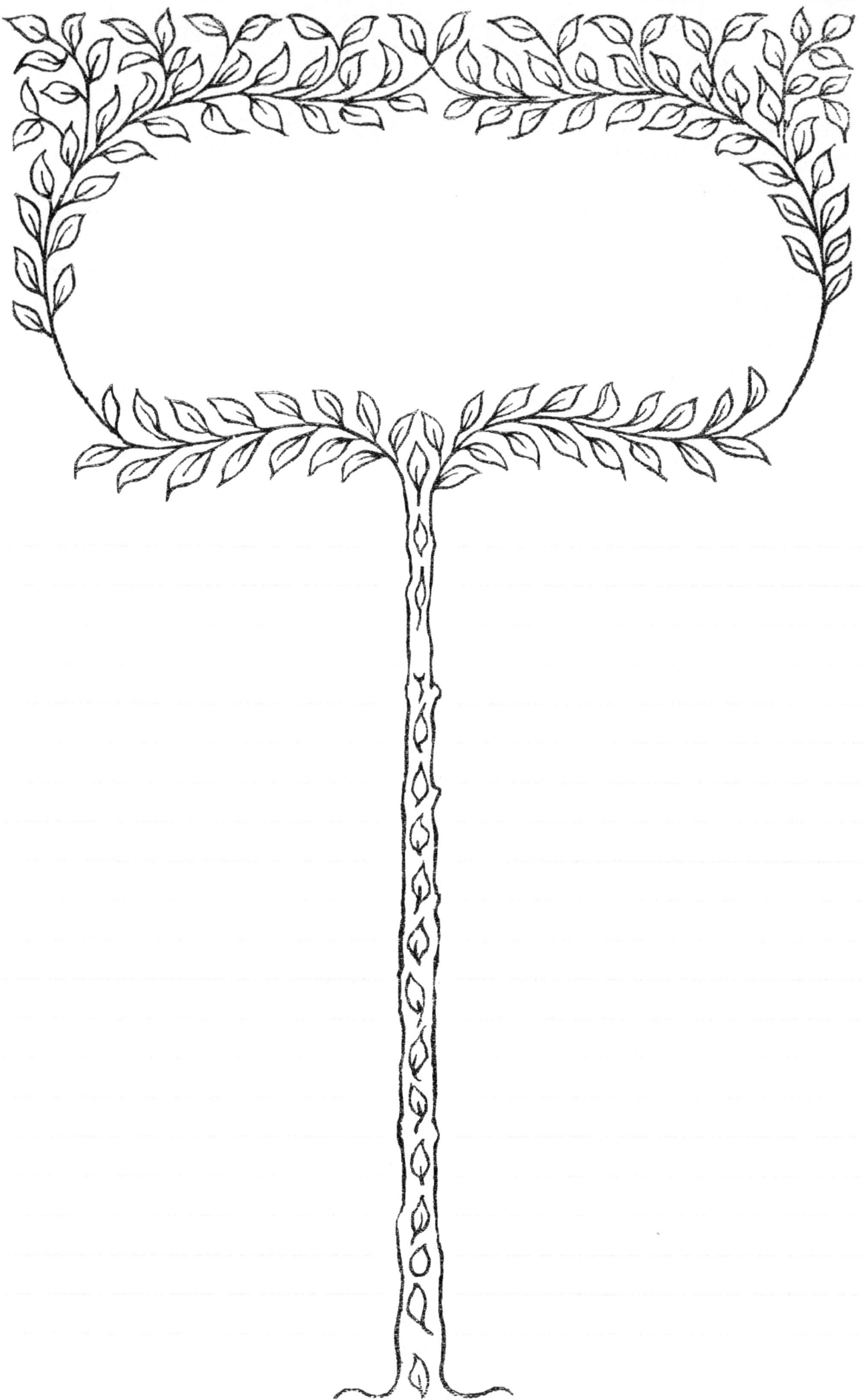

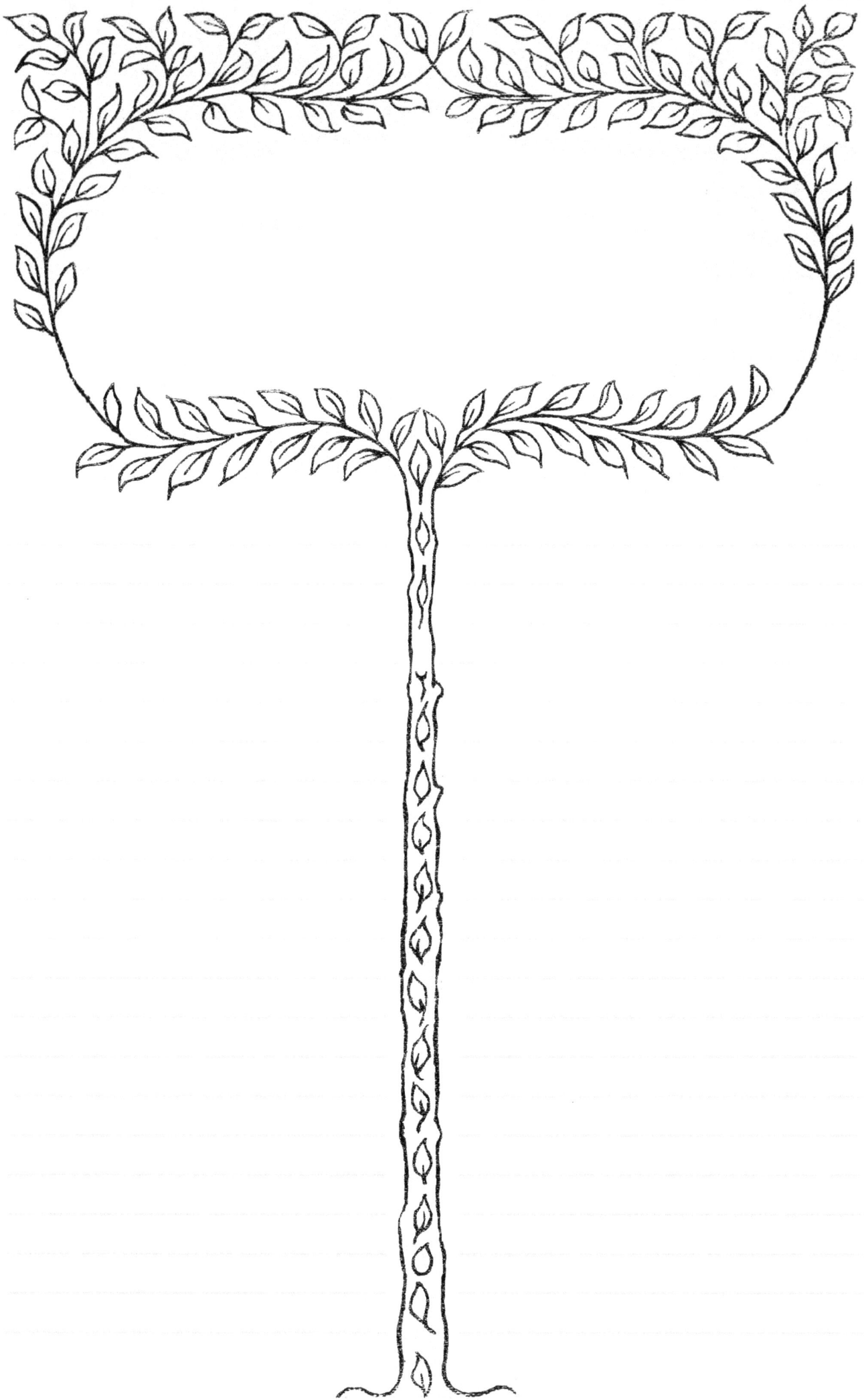

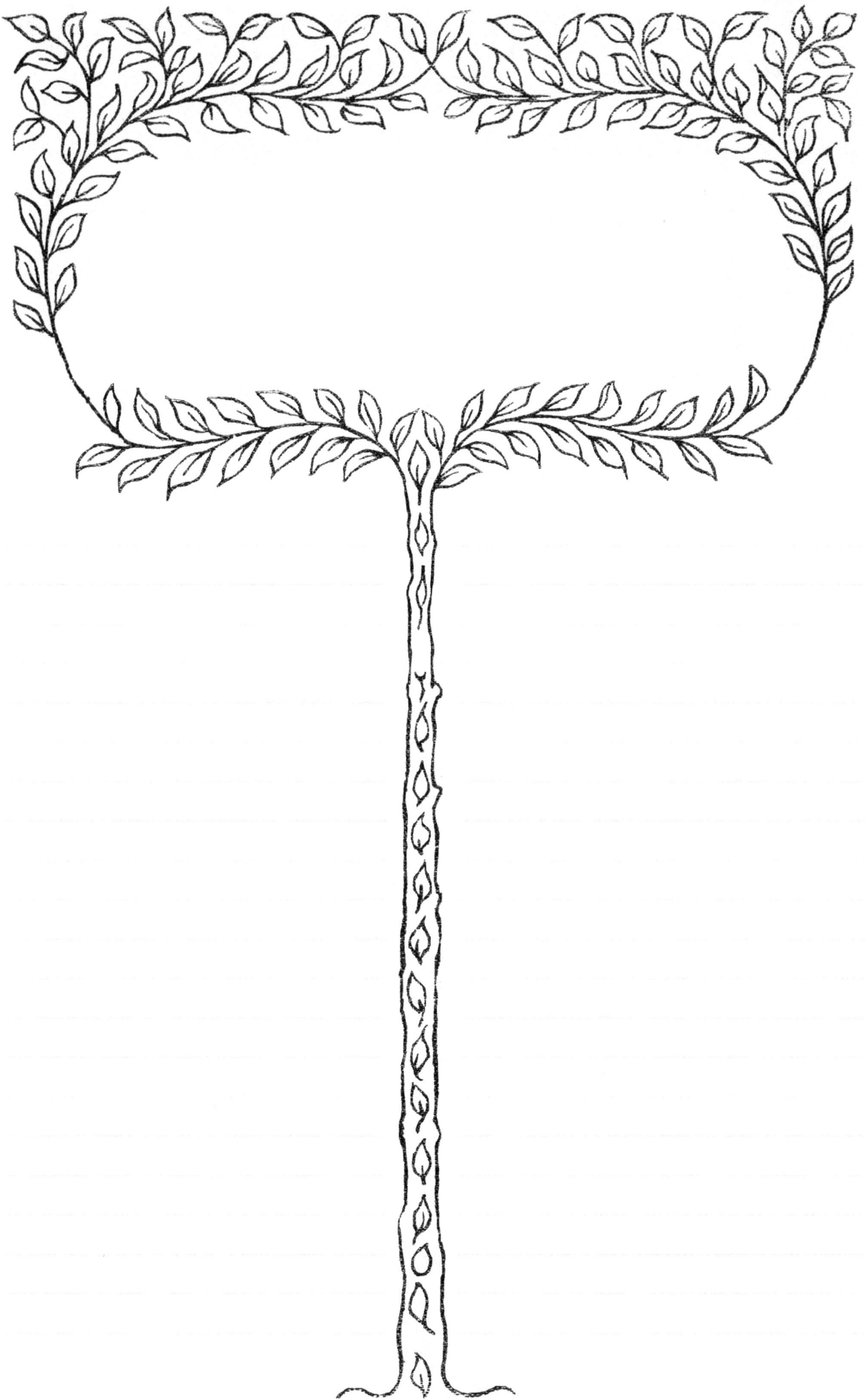

OUR
FAMILY TREE

This   family history
was compiled by
in the year(s)
Valuable contributions were made by:

This book was designed by the artist Sarah Zar for House Elves Anonymous, a project devoted to creating museum-quality family heirlooms and useful genealogy research materials. S. Zar's website is SarahZar.com.

You can order the family tree poster that matches this book, and purchase additional copies of "Our Family Tree Index" at **HouseElvesAnonymous.com.** Both are available in digital and print format.

COUSIN CHART

OF FAMILY RELATIONSHIPS

ONCE REMOVED = One generation away from you.

% = Shared DNA between you and your blood relative.

					GREAT GREAT GREAT GRANDPARENT 3.125%
				GREAT GREAT GRANDPARENT 6.5%	THIRD GREAT AUNT or UNCLE 3.125%
			GREAT GRANDPARENT 12.5%	GREAT GREAT AUNT or UNCLE 6.5%	1st COUSIN 3x removed 1.563%
		GRANDPARENT 25%	GREAT AUNT or UNCLE 12.5%	1st COUSIN twice removed 3.125%	2nd COUSIN twice removed 0.781%
	PARENT 50%	AUNT or UNCLE 25%	1st COUSIN once removed 6.5%	2nd COUSIN once removed 1.563%	3rd COUSIN once removed 0.391%
YOU ARE HERE	SIBLING 50%	1st COUSIN 12.5%	2nd COUSIN 3.125%	3rd COUSIN 0.781%	4th COUSIN 0.195%
CHILD 50%	NIECE or NEPHEW 25%	1st COUSIN once removed 6.25%	2nd COUSIN once removed 1.563%	3rd COUSIN once removed 0.391%	4th COUSIN once removed 0.0977%
GRANDCHILD 25%	GREAT NIECE or NEPHEW 12.5%	1st COUSIN twice removed 3.125%	2nd COUSIN twice removed 0.781%	3rd COUSIN twice removed 0.195%	4th COUSIN twice removed 0.0488%

IN THESE 12
GENERATIONS...
OF

GEN.	FAMILY RELATIONSHIP	# IN THIS GENERATION	CUMULATIVE	~ BIRTH YEAR
1	First person in tree	1	1	x
2	Parents	2	3	x − 30
3	Grandparents	4	7	x − 60
4	Great-grandparents	8	15	x − 90
5	2 times great-grandparents	16	31	x − 120
6	3 times great-grandparents	32	63	x − 150
7	4 times great-grandparents	64	127	x − 180
8	5 times great-grandparents	128	255	x − 210
9	6 times great-grandparents	256	511	x − 240
10	7 times great-grandparents	512	1023	x − 270
11	8 times great-grandparents	1024	2047	x − 300
12	9 times great-grandparents	2048	4095	x − 330

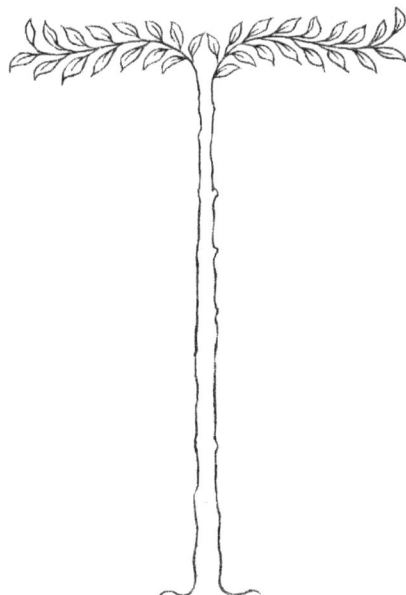

TO BE
CONTINUED...